Fun with Nan and Pop!

by Vaishali Batra

OXFORD
UNIVERSITY PRESS

We go on buses.

This is fun!

We go to the shops.

We pack a bag.

I will get the pink rug.

We sit on a rug.

We rush to check the bugs.

We dig with them.

Then we fill a bucket.

We push the net in.

We chop.

Let me mash!

We chat and hug.

We sing songs.

This is fun!

15

We nap!